LET'S RIDE!

LOWRIDERS

MARIE ROGERS

PowerKiDS press.

NEW YORK

Published in 2022 by The Rosen Publishing Group, Inc.
29 East 21st Street, New York, NY 10010

First Edition

Portions of this work were originally authored by J. Poolos and published as *Wild About Lowriders*. All new material this edition authored by Marie Rogers.

Editor: Kate Mikoley
Book Design: Rachel Rising

Photo Credits: Cover Dmitry Dven/Shutterstock.com; cover, pp. 1, 3, 4, 6, 8, 10, 12, 14, 16, 18, 20, 22, 23, 24 StarLine/Shutterstock.com; cover, p. 1 absemetov/Shutterstock.com; pp. 4, 5 schlol/E+/Getty Images; p. 6 ullstein bild/Contributor/Getty Images; p. 7 Robert Alexander/Contributor/Archive Photos/Getty Images; p. 8 sihuo0860371/iStock/Getty Images Plus; p. 9 Fuse/Corbis/Getty Images; p. 11 Ted Soqui/Contributor/Getty Images; p. 12 Barrett-Jackson/Contributor/Getty Images; p. 13 Andreas Feininger/Contributor/The LIFE Picture Collection/Getty Images; p. 14 Imagesbybarbara/Editorial RF/Getty Images; p. 15 Barcroft Media/Contributor/Getty Images; p. 16 MCCAIG/iStock/Getty Images Plus; p. 17 DOUGBERRY/Editorial RF/Getty Images; p. 18 Stewart Cook/Stringer/Hulton Archive/Getty Images; p. 19 Ted Soqui/Contributor/Corbis Historical/Getty Images; p. 20 Des-Green/Shutterstock.com; p. 21 CatLane/iStock Unreleased/Getty Images.

Library of Congress Cataloging-in-Publication Data

Names: Rogers, Marie, 1990- author.
Title: Lowriders / Marie Rogers.
Description: New York : PowerKids Press, [2022] | Series: Let's ride! |
Includes index.
Identifiers: LCCN 2020045774 | ISBN 9781725327436 (library binding) | ISBN 9781725327412 (paperback) | ISBN 9781725327429 (6 pack)
Subjects: LCSH: Lowriders–Juvenile literature. |
Automobiles–Customizing–Juvenile literature.
Classification: LCC TL255.2 .R63 2022 | DDC 629.222–dc23
LC record available at https://lccn.loc.gov/2020045774

Manufactured in the United States of America

CPSIA Compliance Information: Batch #CSPK22. For Further Information contact Rosen Publishing, New York, New York at 1-800-237-9932.

CONTENTS

THE LOWDOWN ON LOWRIDERS

The bodies of most cars sit at least 5 inches (13 cm) above the ground. But lowriders aren't like most cars! These cars or trucks have been changed to ride very low to the ground. Lowrider drivers can also raise and lower their cars.

Lowriders often have flashy paint jobs and small gold or **chrome** wheels. Lowrider owners often cover the seats and insides of doors with a soft cloth called velvet. This gives the inside a flashy feel too!

Lowriders can be made from any car, but many are built from cars made in the 1950s, like this Chevrolet Bel Air from 1957.

UP AND DOWN

A system of narrow tubes called hydraulics join a lowrider to its wheels. As several **batteries** push oil through the tubes, the car moves up and down. The driver works **switches** that control the flow of oil to each wheel. The driver can raise and lower the car by turning the switches on and off.

Skilled drivers can make their lowrider bounce, or go up and down, in many different ways. They can raise just the front, back, or either side of a lowrider.

The driver of this lowrider is showing off the car's hydraulics at a parade in Santa Fe, New Mexico.

EYE-CATCHING CARS

If a lowrider's bouncing doesn't catch your eye, its paint job will. These cars are often painted with a shiny paint called flake, made by mixing tiny bits of metal into the paint. Lowrider paint jobs often have flames or thin stripes called pinstripes. Some lowriders even have pictures painted on them.

The wheels on lowriders are smaller than wheels on everyday cars. This way, when the car is lowered, the wheels don't rub against the **fender**.

Lowrider wheels usually have gold or chrome rods called spokes. Spokes connect the middle of the wheel to the edge of the wheel.

A LOOK INSIDE

The best lowriders don't just have flashy outsides—they have flashy insides too! Some owners leave the insides of their cars in their original condition. Others cover them in leather, velvet, or other fancy cloths. Some add pieces of wood to the **dashboards** and doors too.

Whether the inside of a lowrider is **customized** or not, the car usually has a special steering wheel. Modern lowriders also have loud radios with speakers that fit into the **trunks** of the cars.

This lowrider is lined with orange and yellow velvet! The front seat can turn too.

KINDS OF CARS

With the right **mechanic** on the job, almost any car can become a lowrider.

Early lowriders were made from cars from the 1950s, like the Mercury and the Chevrolet Deluxe. Today, Buicks and Cadillacs are also popular choices.

The Chevrolet Impala is a favorite among lowrider fans. It's known for its long trunk and low roof. Many lowriders today are built from Impalas from the 1960s. So many were sold that they don't cost too much today. Plus, builders can easily find spare parts.

The Chevrolet Impala, left, first came out in 1958. It's shown here with a Pontiac Chieftain, right, and a Lincoln Premiere, back.

CULTURE OF THE CARS

Lowrider builders think of their cars as works of art. The builders and painters of the coolest lowriders are well known in lowrider **culture**. The makers of the best hydraulic systems, wheels, and other parts are also very respected.

Lowriders started out in Mexican American communities in the Southwest United States. They later became popular in hip-hop culture. Lowriders were sometimes used in music videos in the 1990s. Today, people all over the world love lowriders.

Lowrider owners take pride in their **unique** creations. This lowrider has more than 600 customized parts!

SHOWING OFF YOUR LOWRIDER

A favorite activity among lowrider drivers is cruising. Cruising means driving a car slowly down the street. Drivers show off their lowriders' cool paint jobs and make them bounce along the way.

Another popular activity for lowrider lovers is the car show. Here, lowrider builders and owners gather to show off their work. Fans come to look at the cars and vote for their favorites. The owner of the car that is judged best in show takes home a trophy, or prize.

These lowriders are being shown off at a car show in San Diego, California. The **hoods** are open so people can get a look at the engines.

CONTEST TIME

Lowrider owners show off their cars' hydraulics in two kinds of **contests**. In hopping contests, each driver tries to bounce his or her car the highest. In dancing contests, drivers complete a list of moves, such as bouncing, turning, and lifting the corners of the car one at a time.

To control the lowriders, some drivers stand outside their car and use switches that are connected to the car by a cable. Others sit in the driver's seat.

This lowrider is taking part in a hopping contest.

LOOKING AT LOWRIDERS

When most people think of lowriders, they think of cars. However, there are also lowrider motorcycles and bicycles. These usually don't use hydraulics, but they are low to the ground and commonly have flashy paint jobs.

Whether it's a bike, motorcycle, or car, it takes great skill and imagination to build a cool lowrider. If you want to see one, ask an adult to help you find car shows in your area. If you're lucky, you might even see a dancing or hopping contest!

Lowrider bicycles have long, low seats, called banana seats. Lowrider motorcycles and bicycles both commonly have high handlebars.

GLOSSARY

battery: A tool that turns chemical energy into electricity.

chrome: A shiny metal used on cars and motorcycles.

contest: An event in which people try to be the best.

culture: The beliefs, arts, and ways of life of a group of people.

customize: To change something to fit someone's wants or needs.

dashboard: Part of the inside of a car or truck that is below the windshield, or front window, and usually has controls on it.

fender: Any of the corner parts of the body of a car, especially those that surround the wheels.

hood: The cover over a car's engine.

mechanic: A person who builds and fixes machines.

switch: A tool that opens, closes, or changes the connections in an electrical circuit.

trunk: The covered part in the back of a car.

unique: One of a kind.

FOR MORE INFORMATION

BOOKS

Doeden, Matt. *Lowriders*. North Mankato, MN: Capstone Press, 2019.

London, Martha, *Lowriders*. Minnetonka, MN: Kaleidoscope Publishing, 2020.

WEBSITES

Cruising Low and Slow: 10 Great Lowriders
auto.howstuffworks.com/10-great-lowriders.htm
Check out pictures and read about some of the cars that make the coolest lowriders.

Lowriders: Cars with Identities
nmaahc.si.edu/explore/manylenses/lowriders
Learn more about lowriding culture on this page from the National Museum of African American History & Culture.

Publisher's note to educators and parents: Our editors have carefully reviewed these websites to ensure that they are suitable for students. Many websites change frequently, however, and we cannot guarantee that a site's future contents will continue to meet our high standards of quality and educational value. Be advised that students should be closely supervised whenever they access the internet.

INDEX

